If YOU Had to Draw a Universe for Me...

If YOU Had to Draw a Universe for Me...

50 Questions About the Universe, Matter and Scientists

Marc Goldberg
Corinne Pralavorio
Sandrine Saison-Marsollier
Michel Spiro

Translation from French:
Rosie Arscott, Lisa Morris-Sobczynska and John Pym

 WS Education

NEW JERSEY · LONDON · SINGAPORE · BEIJING · SHANGHAI · HONG KONG · TAIPEI · CHENNAI · TOKYO

contents

The Universe

Matter

Researchers

Introduction

What was there before the Big Bang? What's inside a black hole? Does space go on forever? Are researchers ordinary people just like everyone else? Can we catch particles? 500 pupils between the ages of 8 and 11 came up with these and many other questions on the themes of matter, the universe, and research. They drew pictures of their own answers before asking a physicist. This book is the result of this artistic and scientific journey.

The drawings were done by children at French and Swiss primary schools in and around Geneva, during a competition organised by the particle physics laboratory, CERN, in 2014. The competition, which was sponsored by the physicist Michel Spiro, gave the children and their teachers the chance to approach scientific investigation through art.

This book brings together the children's questions and artwork, with scientific answers and cultural quotations. It invites us to understand and take part in the dialogue between science, philosophy, and literature.

We would like to thank all the teachers and pupils who participated in this project. The artwork for the first two chapters was provided by the schools of Bernex Luchepelet, Collonge-Bellerive, Ferney-Voltaire Florian, Genève Europe, Gex Vertes Campagnes, Petit-Lancy Tivoli, Saint-Jean-de-Gonville, Troinex, Veyrier Grand-Salève, and Veyrier Pinchat. The final chapter came from Centre Divonne-les-Bains, Farges Roger Vailland, Meyrin: Bellavista/ Champs-Frechets/Livron/Monthoux, Ornex Bois, Péron La Fontaine, Satigny-village, Thoiry Gentianes, and Vernier Ranches II. We would also like to thank James Gillies for supporting the project, as well as François Briard, Laurianne Trimoulla, Tullio Basaglia, and Arnaud Marsollier of CERN and Véronique Casetta-Lapierre from Geneva's Department of Education, Culture, and Sport for their contributions.

The Universe

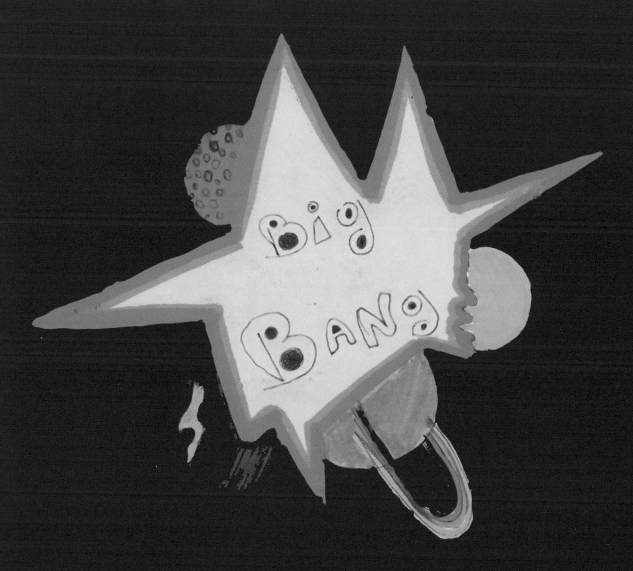

what was the Big Bang?

When we observe the universe, we see that the galaxies are getting further and further apart. This process of expansion is making the universe emptier and colder. The further back in time we look, however, the denser and hotter the universe was. 13.8 billion years ago, it was so dense and hot that all the matter we know today was condensed into a tiny dot. The extremely fast expansion of this little dot, which gave birth to our universe, is what physicists call 'the Big Bang'.

> Before there was earth or sea or the sky that covers everything, Nature appeared the same throughout the whole world: what we call chaos: a raw confused mass, nothing but inert matter, badly combined discordant atoms of things, confused in the one place... Nothing retained its shape, one thing obstructed another, because in the one body, cold fought with heat, moist with dry, soft with hard, and weight with weightless things.

Ovid, *Metamorphoses*, 1st Century AD

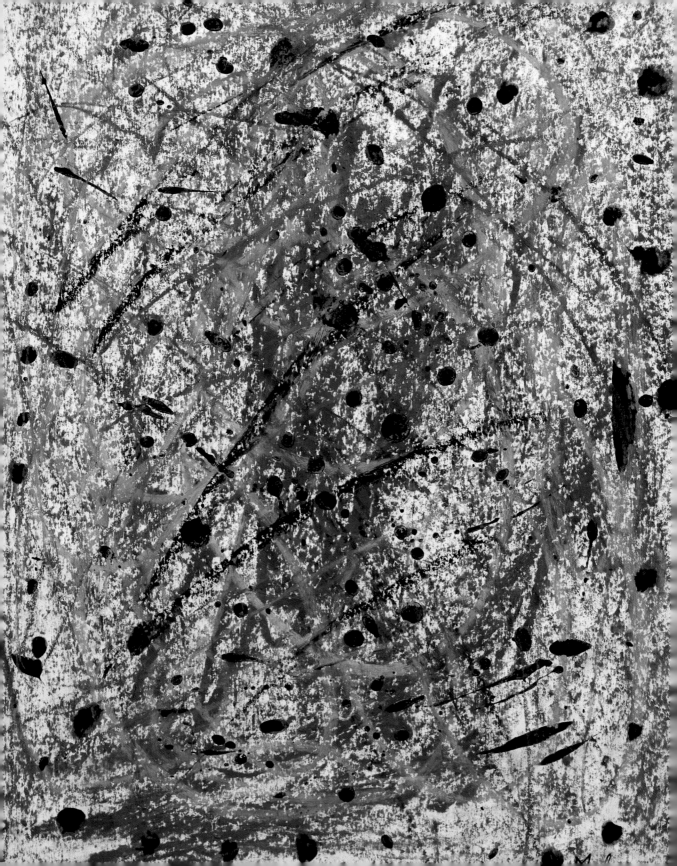

What was there before the Big Bang?

The Big Bang was the sudden expansion of a tiny dot forming a very dense, hot soup of particles. This 'soup' formed the basis for our universe. But where did it come from? This is a vast area of research. We think it came from the vacuum itself. The vacuum, for physicists, is not empty but full of potential, a sort of virtual reality. One of these potentials is thought to have led to our very real universe.

"

The pages are still blank, but there is a miraculous feeling of the words being there, written in invisible ink and clamouring to become visible.

"

Vladimir Nabokov (1899-1977),
Lectures on Literature

Who created the Big Bang?

In principle, physicists never ask the question 'Who created the Big Bang?' Instead, they ask 'How did the Big Bang happen?' Today, we think that the Big Bang exploded from the vacuum. This would mean we all came from the vacuum! For physicists, the vacuum is what's left when all the matter is taken away. Physicists even wonder whether other Big Bangs have happened before or elsewhere.

66

Time will help you through
But it doesn't have the time
To give you all the answers
To the never-ending why.

99

Placebo, *The Never Ending Why*, 2009

what's the smallest thing in the universe? And what's the biggest?

Today, scientists believe that the smallest things in the universe are what we call elementary particles: quarks, electrons, neutrinos, photons, gluons, and a few others. Everything is made up of elementary particles. They are so small that we can't measure their size, or even know if they have size.

The biggest thing is the observable universe — in other words, the part of the universe that is close enough to us for its light to have had time to reach us.

> *Does a world slumber 'neath the starry skies?*
> *Nay, to the heavens do I raise mine eyes,*
> *And, lo, countless worlds and suns do appear,*
> *magnificent in their spot-like veneer!*
> *Their great numbers worldly accounts do defy,*
> *and the tireless soul can but behold the sky.*

Larmartine, *L'Infini dans les Cieux*, 1830
(Translation CERN © 2017)

Does Space go on forever?

Today, we think space goes on forever. This idea comes from recent observations and from the work of the famous physicist, Albert Einstein. Not so long ago, though, scientists thought space was finite, like a balloon. If we move in a straight line across the surface of a balloon, we end up back where we started. It was thought that if we travelled in a straight line across the universe, the same thing would happen. Today, scientists no longer believe this to be the case. But this may not be the final answer...

> Elpino: How is it possible that the universe can be infinite?
> Philotheo: How is it possible that the universe can be finite?
> Elpino: Do you claim that you can demonstrate this infinitude?
> Philotheo: Do you claim that you can demonstrate this finitude?

Giordano Bruno, *On the Infinite, Universe and Worlds*, 1584

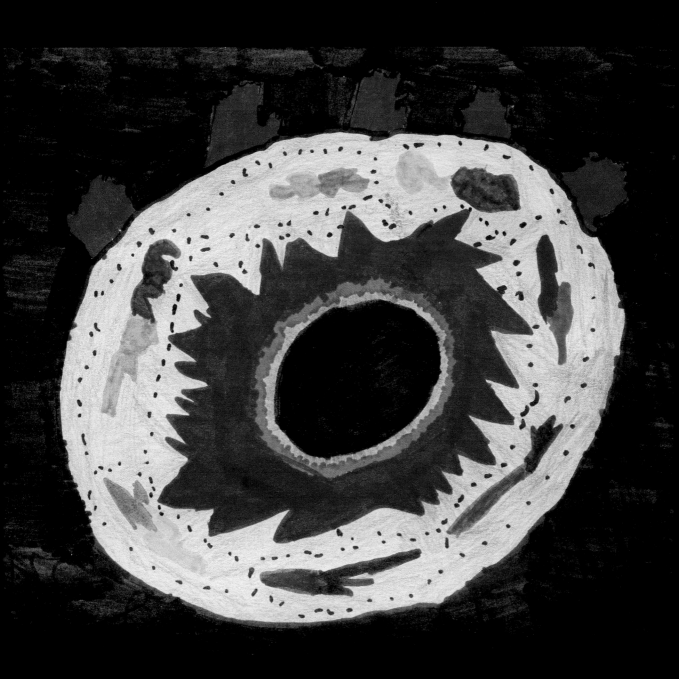

what are stars made of?

Most stars are actually just balls of gas made up of hydrogen and helium. The Sun is just one of the 100 billion stars in the Milky Way, our galaxy. Nuclear reactions take place in the cores of stars, releasing enormous quantities of energy. This energy is carried to the surface, where it's given out as light. This is what makes stars shine.

> Our Sun is a second- or third-generation star. All of the rocky and metallic material we stand on, the iron in our blood, the calcium in our teeth, the carbon in our genes were produced billions of years ago in the interior of a red giant star. We are made of star-stuff.
>
> Carl Sagan, *The Cosmic Connection: An Extraterrestrial Perspective*, 1973

Can a star explode?

Yes, a star can explode at the end of its life. For example, if a star is big enough, the nuclear reactions happening inside it eventually cause iron to be produced in its core. When the mass of iron becomes too great, the core falls apart. This is accompanied by a spectacular explosion that makes the star very bright. This phenomenon is what we call a supernova.

> *One of the first descriptions of a supernova in 1006: A new star appeared, unusual in size, of a brilliant appearance, and striking (to) the eye not without terror. In a wonderful manner this was sometimes contracted, sometimes diffused, and moreover sometimes extinguished. It was seen likewise for three months in the inmost limits of the south, beyond all the constellations which are seen in the sky.*

Hepidannus, *Chronicle of St. Gall Abbey,*
11th Century AD

Why are the Earth and stars round?

It's gravity that makes the Earth and stars round in shape. Gravity is the force that keeps us on Earth. Without it, we would float like astronauts in space. The bigger a planet or a star, the greater its gravity. Earth, the other planets, and stars are especially big. Their gravitational force is so strong that they become round. However, they may have small irregularities on their surface, such as the mountains and craters on the Earth and on the moon. Asteroids, which are much smaller than planets, aren't round.

> *Anaximenes and Anaxagoras and Democritus say that its [the earth's] flatness is responsible for it staying put: for it does not cut the air beneath but covers it like a lid.*

Aristotle (384-322 BC), On the Sky

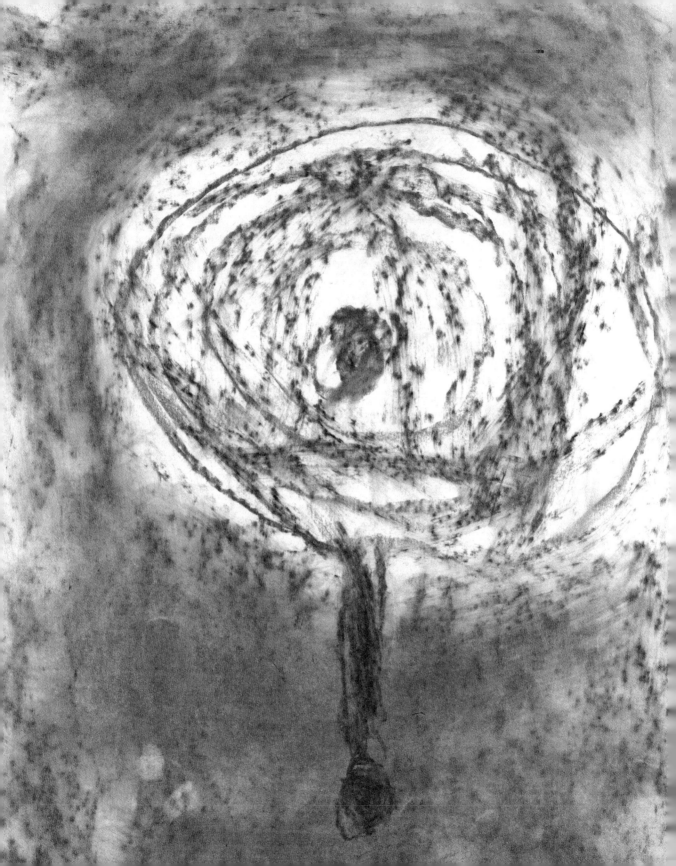

How are black holes detected?

Black holes are so dense that they suck in everything around them. Nothing can escape from them, not even light. We can't see them. So how can we prove that a black hole exists? Indirect evidence and observations are our only clues. For example, we might see a star that seems to be orbiting around nothing. This 'nothing' must be pulling the star in, forcing it into an inescapable orbit. It may therefore be a black hole. Or we might see matter seemingly falling into nothing. Once again, this 'nothing' could well be a black hole.

> A strange rainbow enfolds a sombre hole,
> Stoop of the old chaos whose shadow is the void,
> Spiral that swallows the Worlds and Days!

Gérard de Nerval, *Christ on the Mount of Olives*, 1844

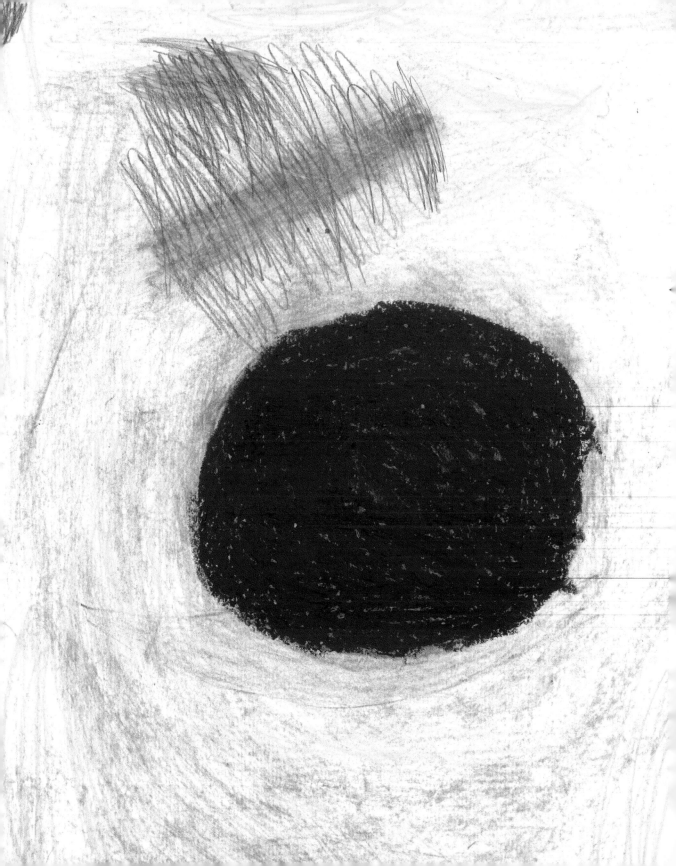

what's inside a black hole?

We don't know! Anything that falls into a black hole is never seen again. We think everything trapped inside a black hole breaks down into elementary particles such as quarks, electrons, and photons. A black hole is like a bottomless pit. But some scientists think these lost particles re-emerge elsewhere in the universe, through a sort of tunnel called a 'wormhole'.

> *In abstraction it creates*
> *A disarming force*
> *And turns the minimum*
> *Into the empire of nought*
>
> *A life-sucking force*
> *Wantonly strikes*
> *Greedily devours*
> *A terrible vortex*
> *To the cold void*
>
> *Monster that chews*
> *Swallows*
> *Digests*
> *But gives nothing back*
>
> *Nothing*
> *No trace*
> *Nor echo*

André Verdet, *Sphère non radieuse*, 1984
(Translation CERN © 2017)

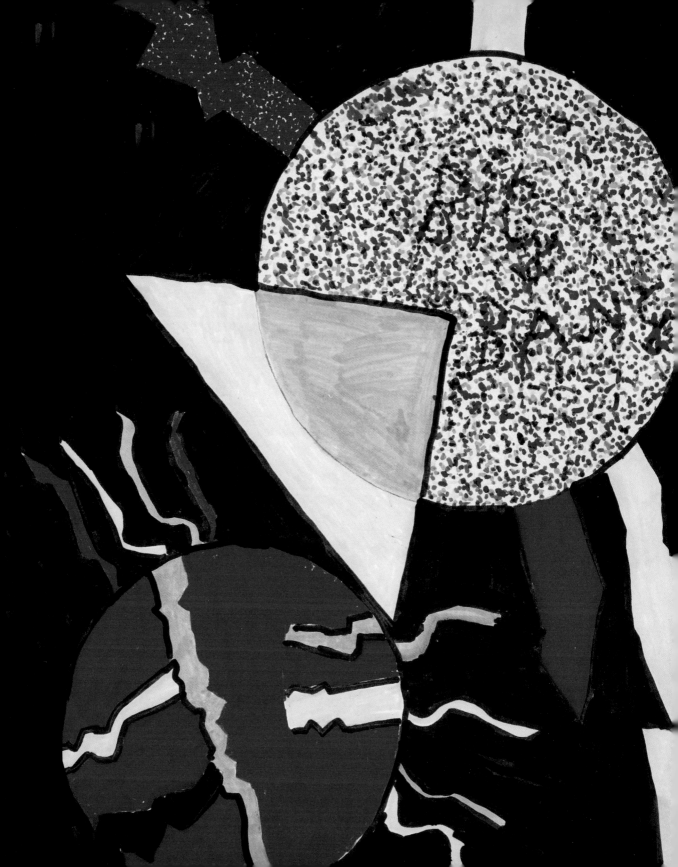

Why does the Earth orbit the Sun? Why don't we feel it turning?

Gravity pulls the Earth towards the Sun, making it turn. Because the Sun is over 300,000 times heavier than the Earth, it is more or less fixed and doesn't move. This is why we orbit it rather than the other way round.

We don't notice the Earth moving because we're moving with it. It's exactly like travelling on a train. When its speed is constant, we don't realise we're moving unless we look out of the window.

In theory one is aware that the earth revolves, but in practice one does not perceive it, the ground upon which one treads seems not to move, and one can live undisturbed. So it is with Time in one's life.

Marcel Proust, *In the Shadow of Young Girls in Flowers*, 1919

Why is the Earth's interior hot when space is cold?

The Earth's interior is hot because the matter there is very dense. The nuclear reactions happening there release heat, warming the centre of the Earth. In contrast, space is almost empty, which makes it cold. The emptier a place is, the colder it is. Space is so empty that temperature has little meaning there.

66

The sensation of falling off the round, turning world. into cold, blue-black space.

99

Elizabeth Bishop,
In the Waiting Room, 1976

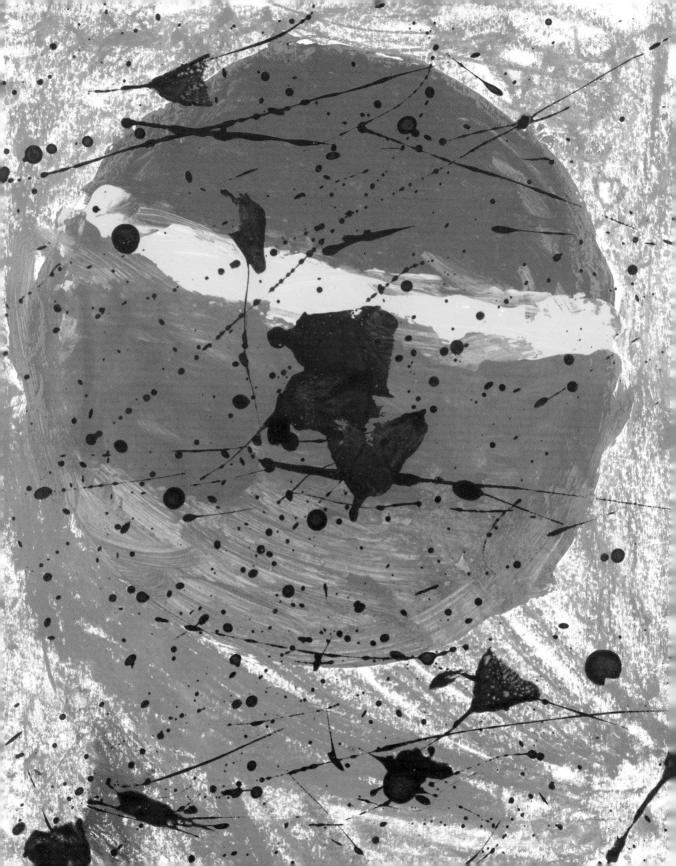

How do you know how long the Sun will live?

A shining star is like a moving car: it shines for as long as its fuel lasts. A star's fuel is hydrogen. The brighter it shines, the more hydrogen it uses. When all of its fuel has been used up, it stops shining and dies. If physicists know a star's luminosity (its fuel consumption) and mass (its fuel stores), they can calculate its lifespan. This is how they've calculated the Sun's lifespan and predicted that it will die in 4.5 billion years.

> *I had a dream, which was not all a dream.*
> *The bright sun was extinguish'd, and the stars*
> *Did wander darkling in the eternal space,*
> *Rayless, and pathless, and the icy earth*
> *Swung blind and blackening in the moonless air.*

Lord Byron, *Darkness*, 1816

Is the Sun growing or shrinking?

Today, the Sun has a radius of 700,000 km. Like all stars, it shines because it's burning up its hydrogen. It has been like this for the last 4.5 billion years. Always the same brightness, always the same size. But physicists have calculated that in another 4.5 billion years, the Sun will have burned up all of its hydrogen. It will then swell, become a red giant, and surround the Earth. Then its outer layers (or 'envelope') will expand and its core will become a dead star, or white dwarf, with a radius of just 7,000 km, the same size as the Earth. This dead star will then cool down for all eternity.

> *The man who ponders the Heavens often marvels at the ghostly after-glow he can see of suns that exist no more, in the illusion of the Universe.*

Villiers de L'Isle-Adam, *L'Ève future*, 1886
(Translation CERN © 2017)

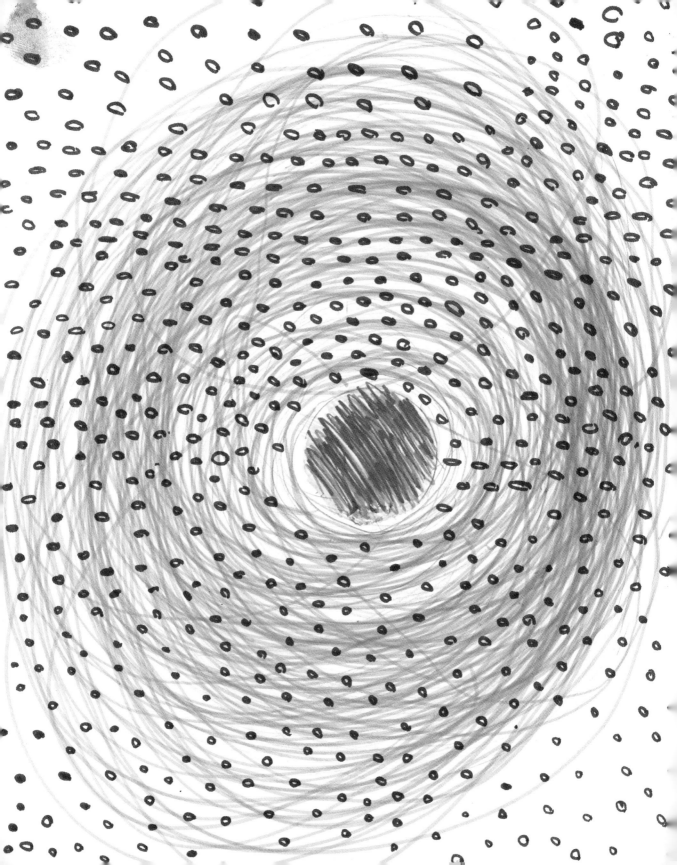

Why is the sun hot?

The Sun started life as an enormous cloud that contracted, becoming so dense that nuclear reactions began inside of it. These reactions release an enormous amount of heat, raising the temperature of the Sun's core to several million degrees. This heat spreads out from the centre of the Sun to its surface, which reaches 6,000 degrees.

> This foster-father, enemy of chlorosis,
> Makes verses bloom in the fields like roses;
> He makes cares evaporate toward heaven,
> And fills with honey hives and brains alike.
> He rejuvenates those who go on crutches
> And gives them the sweetness and gaiety of girls,
> And commands crops to flourish and ripen
> In those immortal hearts which ever wish to bloom!

Baudelaire, *The Sun*, 1857

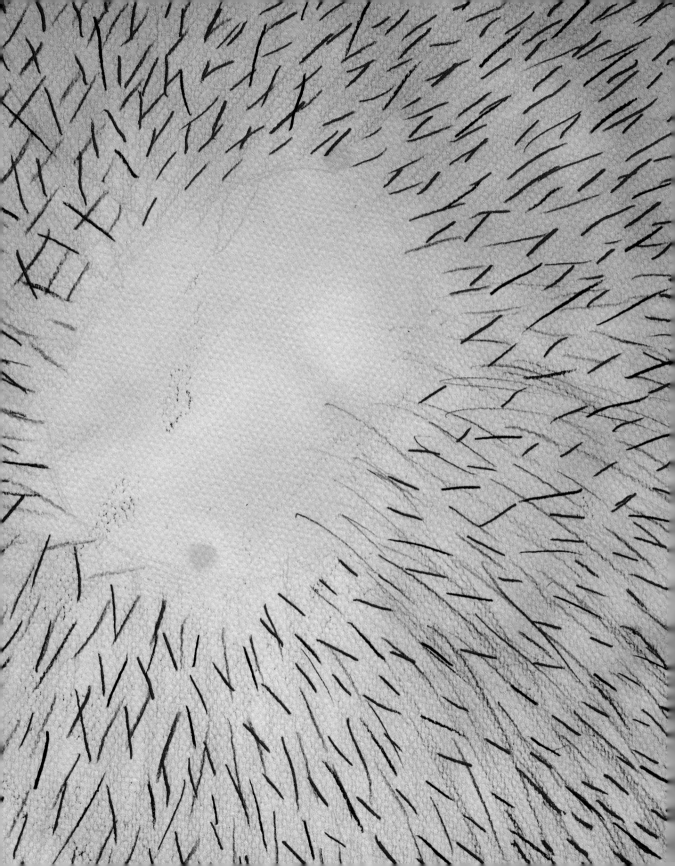

What will happen to the universe when the Sun is no longer there?

When the Sun reaches the end of its life in 4.5 billion years, it will expand and become a red giant. It will then surround the Earth, before contracting again and becoming a white dwarf that will cool down for all eternity. What will become of the human race? Perhaps it will already be extinct. Perhaps it will have moved to a different planet near another star. We don't know! We can only be sure that the universe will continue to evolve.

> *Some say the world will end in fire,*
> *Some say in ice.*
> *From what I've tasted of desire*
> *I hold with those who favor fire.*
> *But if it had to perish twice,*
> *I think I know enough of hate*
> *To say that for destruction ice*
> *Is also great*
> *And would suffice.*

Robert Frost, *Fire and Ice*, 1920

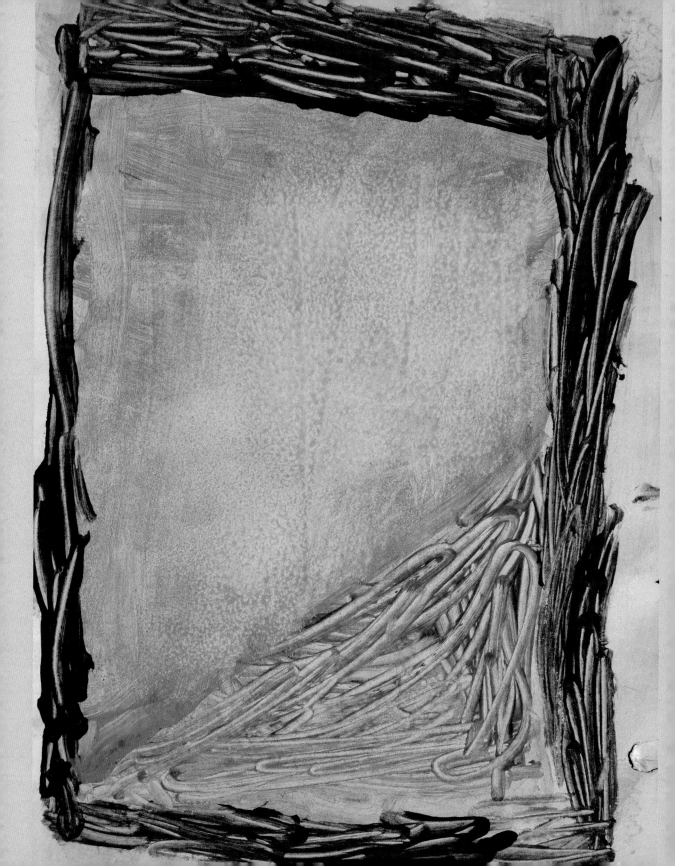

Why can there be only three dimensions?

When we look at an object, we see it in three dimensions: depth, width, and height. These are the three dimensions of our universe. But there's also a fourth dimension — time — which describes its evolution. Why aren't there fewer dimensions? Well, it's hard to imagine two-dimensional, flat living things evolving in a flat space. Could there be more than four dimensions? Some theories predict that there may be ten dimensions, six of which are so small that we haven't yet discovered them. Four, ten, perhaps even more — this is a question we can't yet answer.

> *Oh but it's cold here in the spaces of the Calabi-Yau*
> *Much colder than the seas where fishing for cod we go*
> *It's why the dimensions huddle together to keep warm*
> *Eleven of them (including time), each with their own form.*

Jacques Réda, *Physique amusante*, 2009
(Translation CERN © 2017)

If You Had to Draw a Universe for Me...

what's the most beautiful thing in the universe?

In their work, scientists don't take account of beauty as we generally understand it. They use other criteria to explain the laws of nature and write their theories. However, the theories on which they all agree tend to be the most elegant ones. For scientists, elegance and beauty mean symmetry and simplicity. Symmetry represents perfection and simplicity is very important to the sharing of knowledge.

> *Mathematics, rightly viewed, possesses not only truth, but supreme beauty — a beauty cold and austere, like that of sculpture, without appeal to any part of our weaker nature, without the gorgeous trappings of painting or music, yet sublimely pure, and capable of a stern perfection such as only the greatest art can show.*

Bertrand Russell, *The Study of Mathematics,* 1902

Have scientists found life in space?

Scientists haven't yet found life in space, either in the meteorites that fall to Earth or on the other planets in our solar system. Could there once have been life on Mars? For several years now, scientists have been finding thousands of other planets orbiting stars other than the Sun. Perhaps there could be life on one of them? Scientists are studying these planets for evidence of the conditions necessary for life as we know it on Earth. For example, they're looking for oxygen and hydrogen, the parts that make up water. We know that liquid water played a basic and important role in the emergence of life on Earth. Watch this space.

So many Suns, so many Earths, and every one of them stock'd with so many Herbs, Trees and Animals, and adorn'd with so many Seas and Mountains!

Christian Huygens, *Cosmotheoros*, 1698

Does the Vacuum in space ever end?

Vacuum is what's left when everything has been removed and not even a single particle remains. We can only imagine it. We can't create it, even in a tiny box. But, for physicists, this vacuum isn't empty. They think that even if everything is removed, something will always remain. They call this the 'quantum vacuum'. In this vacuum, so the theory goes, phenomena called fluctuations create virtual particles that appear for a fleeting moment before disappearing without a trace. This vacuum is never-ending. It has always existed and it is the source of our entire universe.

> The vacant interstellar spaces,
> the vacant into the vacant.

T. S. Eliot, *East Cocker*, 1940

Matter

A dive into the infinitesimally small and the infinitely large!

What are we made of? Where did the universe come from? How will it evolve? Using machines more powerful than ever, physicists have been able to discover smaller and smaller constituents of matter. These tiny pieces of matter are called particles. Physicists have also increased our knowledge of the forces that bind these particles together.

PARTICLES

Matter is like a set of Russian dolls. We, and everything around us, are composed of molecules. Molecules consist of atoms, and atoms of a nucleus surrounded by electrons. The nucleus is in turn composed of protons and neutrons. Protons and neutrons are made up of quarks. These are the smallest building blocks of matter that we know of today.

Three particles (two types of quarks and an electron) are all that's needed to create ordinary matter. But physicists have discovered other, heavier quarks, as well as other, more massive particles related to the electron.

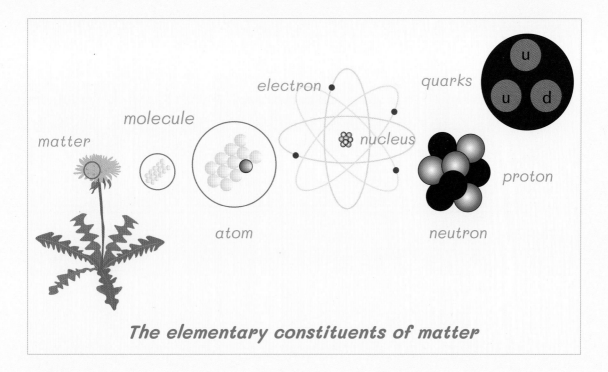

The elementary constituents of matter

FORCES

The forces acting between particles are what ensure that the Sun shines, the Earth spins and objects stay put or fall to the ground. Four forces govern our universe:

⊗ Gravity, which keeps us on the Earth and causes the planets to orbit the stars;

⊗ The electromagnetic force, which is the source of electricity and makes magnets attract and repel each other;

⊗ The weak nuclear force, which is responsible for radioactivity and the emission of particles by materials (also called 'particle decay');

⊗ The strong nuclear force, which holds the parts of atomic nuclei together very strongly.

THE BIG BANG

The entire universe that we're able to observe is thought to have come from a very dense, hot point that suddenly expanded. This was the Big Bang. Physicists study the infinitesimally small with huge machines called particle accelerators, which produce particle collisions at very high energies. These collisions recreate the conditions that existed just after

*The emergence of
protons and neutrons:*
0.01 milliseconds

*The evolution of the
universe, from the Big
Bang to the present day.
Particles of matter
grouped together to
form atoms. These atoms
formed increasingly
complex structures to
create the universe in
which we live.*

BiG BANG

the Big Bang, in an infinitesimal space and for a fleeting moment. This is why understanding the infinitesimally small also allows us to understand the infinitely large: the universe, its emergence, and its evolution.

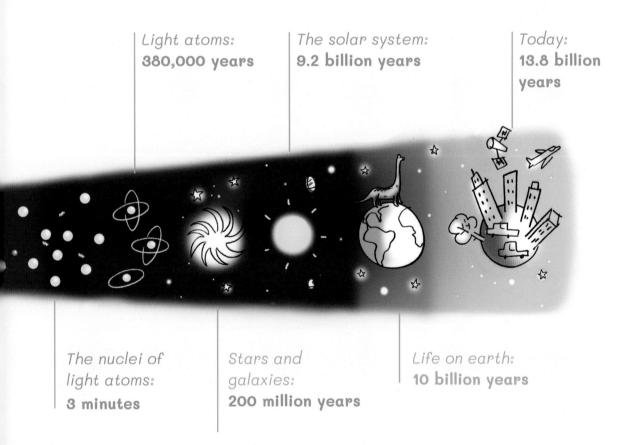

Light atoms:
380,000 years

The solar system:
9.2 billion years

Today:
13.8 billion years

The nuclei of light atoms:
3 minutes

Stars and galaxies:
200 million years

Life on earth:
10 billion years

How can we see particles?

We can't see particles with the naked eye because they're extremely small. We usually use microscopes to look at very small things, but even the most powerful microscopes can't help us to see elementary particles. We need particle accelerators and detectors to be able to observe them. Accelerators accelerate particles to very high speeds and collide them with the matter we want to study. Detectors record the tracks that the particles leave during these collisions. Studying these tracks helps us to understand what matter is made of. But accelerators do more than just probe matter. The collisions they produce can create new particles, which can also be identified by the detectors.

> *He was examining most attentively a heap of black coagulated ashes, with a hollow imprint. It looked like a fragment of a statue mould, broken in the casting. An artist's practiced eye would have easily recognized in it the outline of a beautiful bosom, and of a hip as pure in style as that of a Greek statue.*
>
> Théophile Gautier, Arria Marcella, A Souvenir of Pompeii, 1852

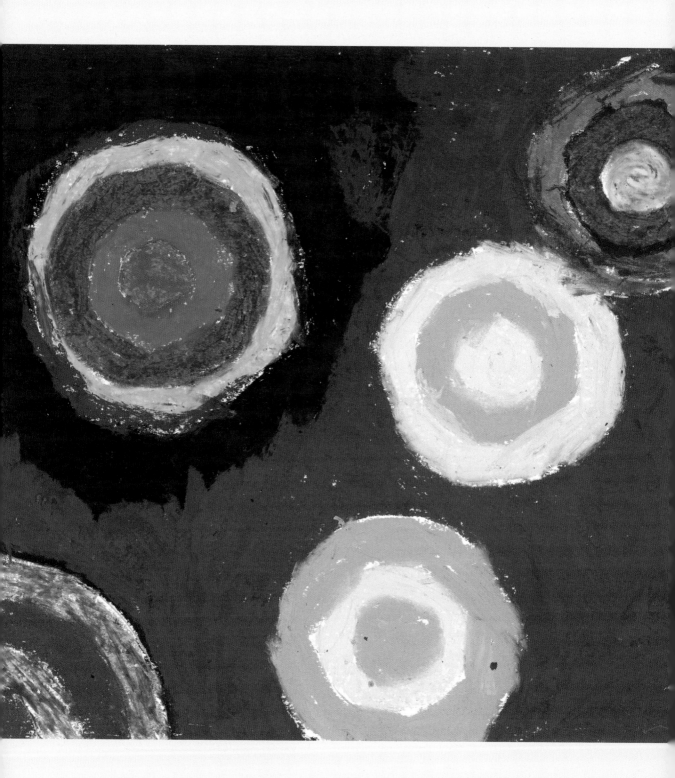

How can we identify different types of particles?

Elementary particles are so tiny that they're invisible to the naked eye. However, when they pass through matter, they leave tracks behind them. We identify them using detectors made of magnets and many different materials. Different types of particles leave different clues in the layers of material. By piecing these clues together, we can tell one particle apart from another.

" In the grass laden by the risen dew, lay the immaculate imprint of her big talon: aligned at 120° are three strong, unequal talons with a last, stunted one at the rear. "

Marcel Aymé, *La Vouivre*, 1943
(Translation CERN © 2017)

Are particles living things?

Living things are so described because they are born, reproduce, age, and die. They belong to living species, which are made up of individuals that are all different and which themselves evolve. Is the same true for particles? We could say that particles are born during collisions and that they die either by decaying into other particles or by colliding with other particles and disappearing. However, unlike living things, they don't age, but remain exactly the same from the moment they're created until the moment they cease to exist. They belong to species that do not evolve and whose individuals are all the same. Particles are therefore not living things according to the traditional meaning of the concept.

> "
>
> *The particles that form matter possess the power to build, to produce structures of increasing complexity and even to reproduce themselves. From the simplest organisms to the human being, all have a host of integrations, levels and discontinuities. But without the slightest break in the composition of the objects or in the reactions occurring within them. Without the slightest change of 'essence'.*
>
> "

François Jacob, *La logique du vivant*, 1970
(Translation CERN © 2017)

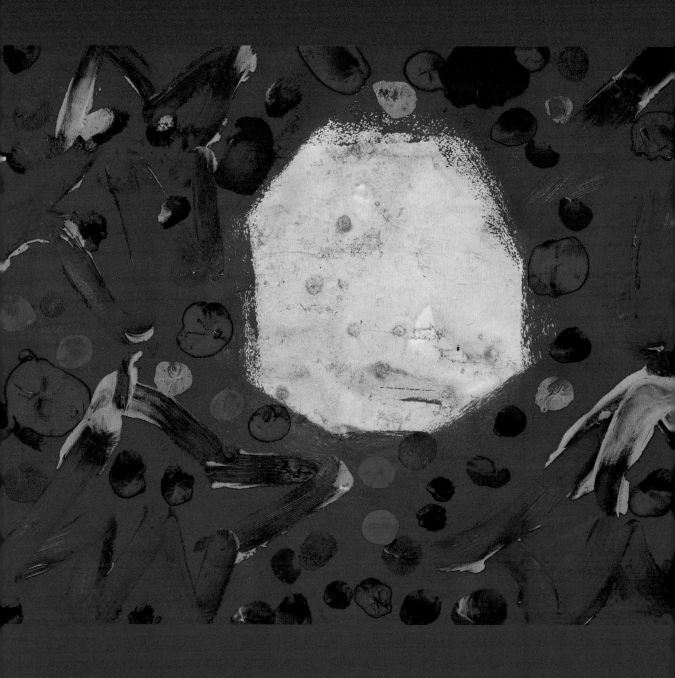

Do particles travel between countries?

Particles don't travel between countries, because when they come across matter, they are slowed down and absorbed. They travel in a straight line, so they can't avoid coming into contact with matter. Even air slows them down, as air is also matter. Only the particles we call neutrinos are able to pass through matter, because they hardly notice it as they travel. But if particles are thrown into empty space, they can travel long distances. Some particles actually come to Earth from space: in this case, we call them 'cosmic rays'.

> Above the lakes, above the vales,
> The mountains and the woods, the clouds, the seas,
> Beyond the sun, beyond the ether,
> Beyond the confines of the starry spheres,
>
> My soul, you move with ease,
> And like a strong swimmer in rapture in the wave
> You wing your way blithely through boundless space
> With virile joy unspeakable.

Baudelaire, *Elevation*, 1857

Are particles hot or cold?

Particles are neither hot nor cold. Assembled into atoms, they form the molecules that make up matter. The more these molecules move about, the hotter the matter becomes. For example, the molecules in hot milk move quicker than those in cold milk. Heat is a sign of movement, cold a sign of stillness.

> *What Power art thou who from below*
> *Hast made me rise unwillingly and slow*
> *From beds of everlasting snow?*
> *See'st thou not how stiff and wondrous old,*
> *Far unfit to bear the bitter cold,*
> *I can scarcely move or draw my breath?*
> *Let me, let me freeze again to death.*

John Dryden, *The Cold Song in King Arthur from Henry Purcell, 1691*

can we catch particles?

Yes, we can catch particles. All we need to do is trap them by placing obstacles in their path. If the particles have a lot of energy, we need a lot of obstacles — in other words, a lot of matter. We can also catch them in another way: by slowing them down and trapping them with magnets.

However, some particles are harder to catch than others because they interact less with matter. This is the case for neutrinos, which are hardly ever caught.

> *Finally his last great passion: will-o'-the-wisps. He wanted to find a way of catching and keeping them, and with this aim in view we would spend nights wandering about our cemetery, waiting for one of those vague lights to go up among the mounds of earth and grass, when he would try to draw it towards us, make it follow us and then capture it, without its going out.*

Italo Calvino, *The Cloven Viscount*, 1952

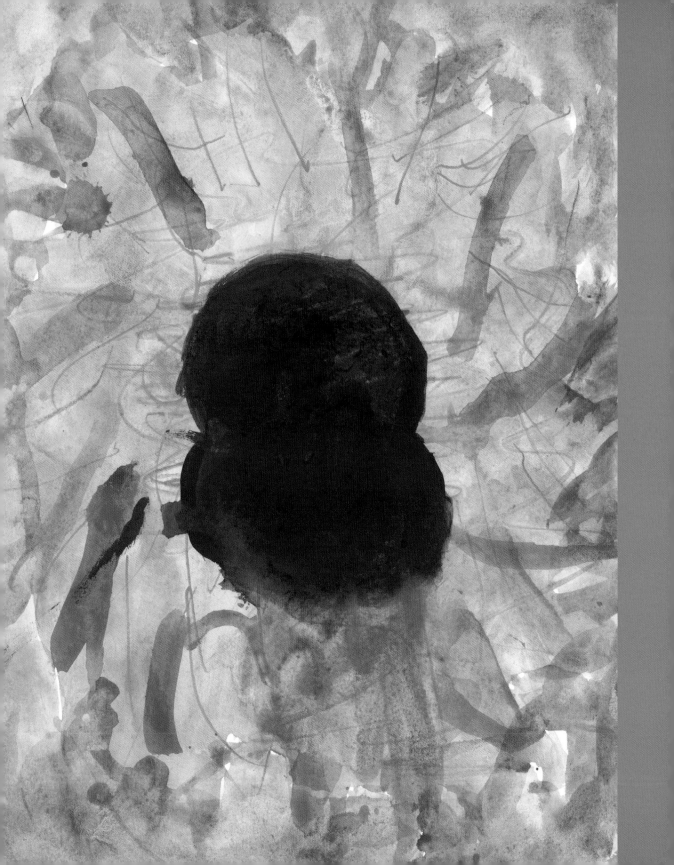

Are any particles dangerous to humans?

Particles are neither completely dangerous nor beneficial to humans. It all depends on how we use them. For example, we can use particles to destroy tumours in the eye or the brain. We can use them to produce images of the human body. They can be used to sterilise foods, especially in tin cans. But particles can also be harmful, causing lesions and tumours if the body's exposed to them for too long. This is because of radioactivity.

> *I also saw survivors and those who were in the wombs of the women of Hiroshima. A beautiful child who, upon turning around, is blind in one eye. A girl looking at her burned face in the mirror. A blind girl with twisted hands playing the zither.*

Marguerite Duras, *Hiroshima mon amour, 1969*

Where did the first particles come from?

It's generally thought that the first particles came from the Big Bang. In a billionth of a billionth of a billionth of a billionth of a second, the energy of the Big Bang transformed into a soup of particles. These particles were all the same and had no mass. The vacuum then underwent many transformations and the different types of particle that we know appeared. These then came together to create protons and neutrons, then nuclei and atoms. The particles that surround us and of which we're made were created 13.8 billion years ago. So, in a way, you could say we are as old as the universe.

"

Chaos gave birth to Erebos and black Night; then Erebos mated with Night and made her pregnant and she in turn gave birth to Ether and Day.

"

Hesiod, *Theogony, VIIIth Century BC*

How many particles are we made of?

The matter of our bodies is composed of molecules (which are formed of atoms), and each atom is made up of even smaller particles: protons, neutrons, and electrons. Our bodies comprise around a billion billion billion protons, neutrons, and electrons. It's hard to imagine such a gigantic figure. The exact number of particles in our body depends on our weight. The heavier we are, the greater the number of particles in our body.

The human body is the best picture of the human soul.

Wittgenstein, *Philosophical Investigations, 1953*

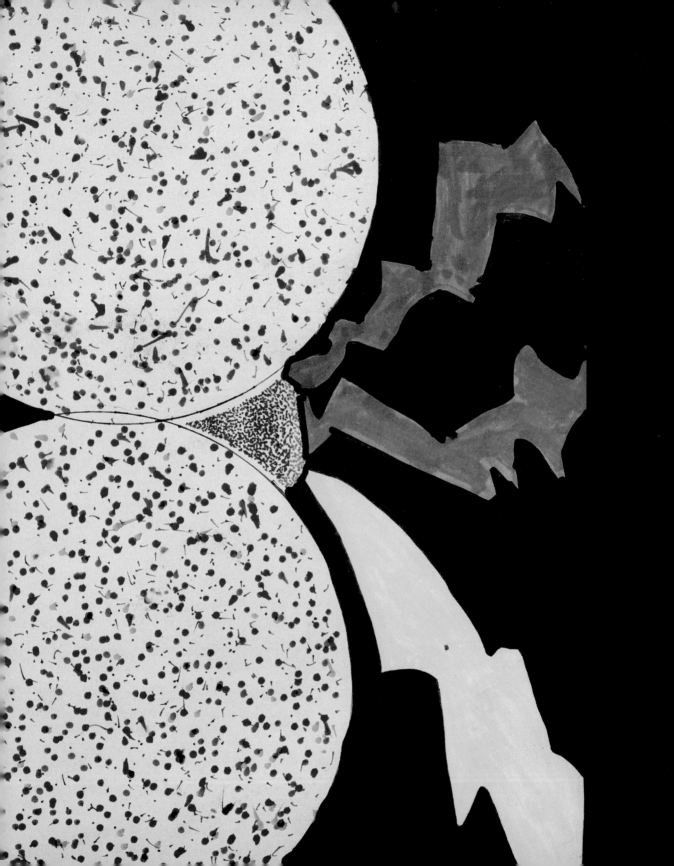

Do particles grow as we grow?

Particles don't grow. However, when we swallow food and drink, the number of particles in our body increases. This is why we get taller and bigger. Both adults and children are constantly absorbing billions and billions of atoms every second, just by breathing. The make-up of our bodies is therefore continuously changing. It's thought that during our lifetime, we'll have absorbed atoms that at one time or another were part of the bodies of living things that came before us.

Does not the body thrive and grow
By food of twenty years ago?
And, had it not been still supplied,
It must a thousand times have died.

Jonathan Swift,
Birthday Poems to Stella, 1726-1727

Do things exist that aren't made of particles?

If we take 'things' to mean things that are made of matter, then no, they're all composed of particles, mainly quarks and electrons. Even light's made of particles, like photons! So, does this mean that everything's made of particles? Yes, but thoughts, ideas, and laws can be considered to be part of the world, and they aren't made of particles! So what is the world of thoughts, ideas, and laws? Is it a separate world, or is it just something that our brains, which themselves are made of particles, have created to help us see and understand the world better?

> *By convention sweet and by convention bitter,*
> *by convention colour;*
> *but in reality atoms and void.*

Democritus (460-370 BC), Fragments

Amine

If the air is made of particles and water is also made of particles, why do I float in water but not in air?

Water, air, and we ourselves are all made up of the same kinds of particles assembled into atoms and molecules. But these molecules are arranged differently from one substance or material to another, and this makes all the difference. Air molecules are more spread out than water molecules, which makes air less dense than water. An object only floats on water or in air if it's density is lesser than theirs. Our bodies are a little less dense than water, but are much denser than air. This is why we float in water but not in the air.

> " Angels... wear the wings for style, but they travel any distance in an instant by wishing. The wishing-carpet of the Arabian Nights was a sensible idea — but our earthly idea of angels flying these awful distances with their clumsy wings was foolish. "

Mark Twain,
Captain Stormfield's Visit to Heaven, 1909

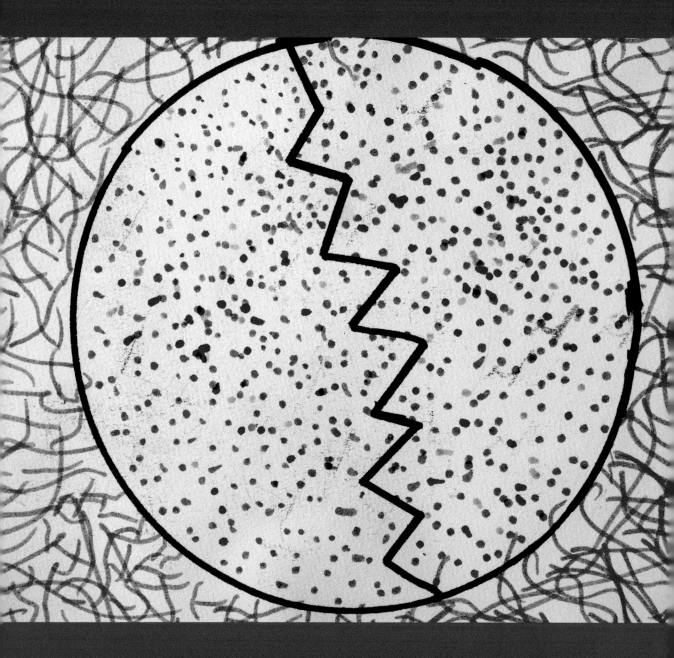

Does matter carry on dividing forever?

Matter is what we and absolutely everything around us are made of. We've studied it and discovered that it's made up of smaller and smaller parts nestled inside each other, like Russian dolls! Physicists have established that the smallest particles of matter are quarks and electrons. They call these 'elementary particles' because they can't break them down any further. They seem to be formed only of themselves! Do smaller building blocks of matter than these exist? We don't know yet. This is a question for the researchers of today and tomorrow.

*Effortlessly, the ape became man
And, a short while later, split the atom.*

Raymond Queneau,
Petite cosmogonie portative, 1950
(Translation CERN © 2017)

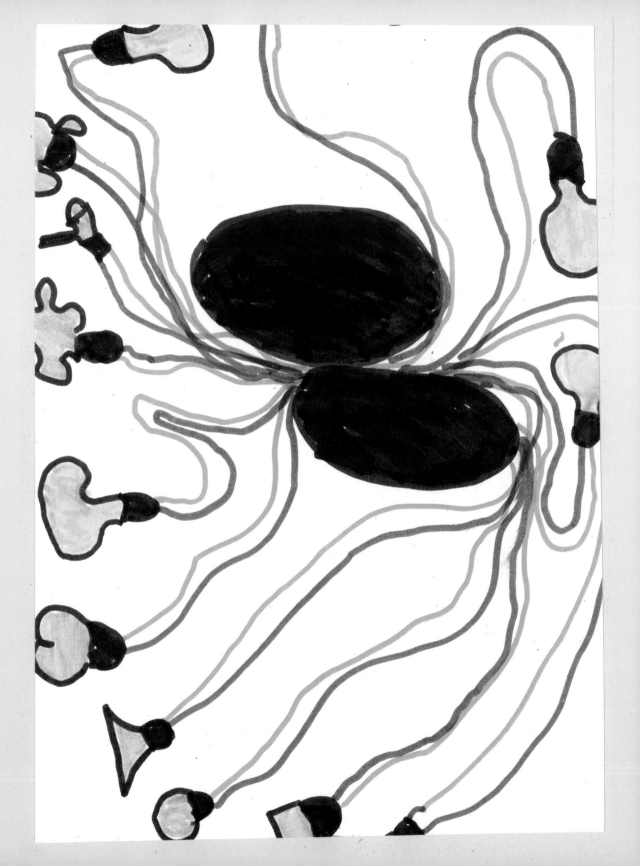

Is there a force capable of breaking electrons?

As far as we can tell today, electrons are elementary. We can't see anything smaller inside them. For us to be able to break something up into pieces, it has to be made up of these pieces in the first place. There don't seem to be any pieces inside electrons, so we can't break them down any further. Perhaps, in the future, we'll discover that electrons are formed of smaller particles after all. We'll then try to find the means, or the strength, to break electrons down into smaller particles. After all, what's true today won't necessarily be true tomorrow!

"

Fair explorers of the cosmos and the infinitesimally small
I've followed you to the edge of the anaemic abyss where all
Below the Planck length will be lost.
I hail your successes and admire the creations
Born of your telescope and computations
and the certain presages you extract
from the entrails of the trembling body
Of matter.

"

Jacques Réda, *Lettre au Physicien*, 2012
(Translation CERN © 2017)

ReSearchers

what do researchers do?

Researchers ask questions about the world we live in and then try to find the answers. Physicists are researchers who are interested in the objects and phenomena of nature, from the smallest parts of matter to the stars and the whole universe itself. Researchers think of questions, design experiments to answer them, perform these experiments, and then examine the results and make calculations. They then draw conclusions to answer their questions. They also use the work of other researchers who preceded them. They often work in teams and in competition with other researchers around the world. This is how they increase the knowledge of humankind. Many other professions also increase knowledge, such as computer scientists and engineers. They all share a passion for their subject and a sense of wonder at the world around them.

" I thought of a labyrinth of labyrinths, of one sinuous spreading labyrinth that would encompass the past and the future and in some way involve the stars. "

Jorge Luis Borges, *Fictions, 1944*

Are researchers ordinary people just like everyone else?

Yes, researchers are just like everyone else: they may or may not have families and hobbies outside work, they have opinions, and they're citizens just like the rest of us. You have to study for a long time to become a researcher, and it's a life choice. Researchers are generally very curious, they're often passionate and amazed by the world, and they love their job. There are all sorts of researchers, all with different talents: inventive or calculative, practical or theoretical, head-in-the-clouds or down-to-earth. But they all feel part of a big family: a family of researchers from all over the world or the heirs of generations of past researchers. Albert Einstein and Marie Curie were two very important researchers who dedicated themselves to their work with a passion, but whose strong beliefs also kept them actively involved in modern life. They left their mark on their century.

> *To drown in the abyss — heaven or hell, who cares? Through the unknown, we'll find the new.*

Baudelaire, *The Voyage*, 1857

Do researchers take holidays?

If a holiday is a chance to do what you want and to dream, then researchers are always on holiday.

If a holiday is a chance to travel, then researchers are on holiday from time to time, because they sometimes travel to meet colleagues, attend conferences, or conduct work.

If a holiday is a chance to relax and have a change of scenery, then yes, researchers definitely need them, just like everyone else. But even when they're on holiday, they can be busy with their research.

Researchers are a bit like artists: they're passionate, and they eat, sleep, and breathe their passion.

" The fairest thing we can experience is the mysterious. It is the fundamental emotion that stands at the cradle of true art and true science. "

Albert Einstein, *The World As I See It, 1949*

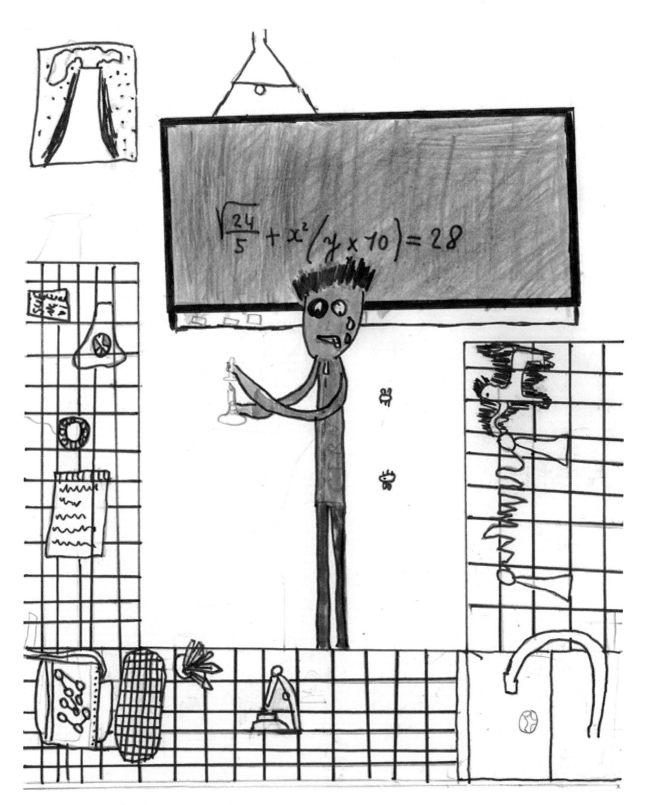

can researchers fail in their experiments?

Yes, an experiment can fail in many ways:

- The experiment was designed to test an incorrect hypothesis! But of course, the researcher didn't know that. The experiment hasn't really failed, because it's shown us that the hypothesis was wrong and that we need to look elsewhere. Sometimes, it can produce an unexpected result.

- The experiment takes longer than expected and another team somewhere else in the world completes it first! In this case, the first experiment can be used to test the other team's results.

- An error has occurred during the experiment and has produced incorrect results or no result at all. It will therefore be corrected by other researchers.

In all cases, a failed experiment is still helpful. Analysing the causes of the failure allows us to improve the way we work. As a result, the researcher will approach future experiments with more knowledge and skill.

Gently make hast, of Labour not afraid;
A hundred times consider what you've said.

Boileau, *The Art of Poetry*, 1674

What's the common language of physicists?

The true common language of physicists is argumentation, expressed through words and mathematics. This 'language' allows them to describe physics phenomena and to try to explain the workings of nature. Understanding and using this language requires many years of study. But the practical language of physicists working together in big laboratories all over the world is English. It's in this language that they write their articles and share their research at conferences. However, at the beginning of the twentieth century, the language used by physicists, chemists, and biologists was German. For centuries before that, it was Latin. In the future, who knows? English might well be replaced by another language.

> *My life will end with a*
> *I am b-a*
> *I ask cb-a*
> *I estimate feast days d/cb-a*
> *My predictions of the future de/cb-a*

Benjamin Péret, *Vingt-six points à préciser,*
Le Grand jeu, 1928 (Translation CERN © 2017)

How many years of study does it take to become a physicist?

To begin a career as a physicist, you need a PhD, which requires at least six years of study after high school. If you want to become and remain a great physicist, you continue to learn even after you have a PhD. Knowledge progresses, and we must progress with it! But anyone can take an interest in and even contribute to physics, at any time and at any age. You just need to be curious.

On the last words of Jacques Monod, winner of the Nobel Prize for Medicine and Director of the Pasteur Institute:

In a first whisper, Mr Monod murmured:
Odette... Pasteur... Jean...
And then, very softly, barely audible:
I'm trying to understand...

Madeleine Brunerie,
Cinquante-huit ans à l'Institut Pasteur,
Vingt-deux ans près de Jacques Monod, 2008
(Translation CERN © 2017)

What's CERN looking for?

What is the matter that surrounds us made of? How did it form? These are the subjects studied at CERN, the European Organization for Nuclear Research, based in Geneva, Switzerland. To carry out this research, physicists have built particle accelerators and detectors. These huge machines allow us to study matter. Physicists can then understand what it's made of and how it formed.

> **Empedocles wrote the following on the four elements (fire, air, earth, water) that form matter:**
>
> *Hear first the four roots of all things: shining Zeus, life-bringing Hera, Aidoneus and Nestis whose tear-drops are a well-spring to mortals.*
>
> Empedocles, *Fragment 6, Vth Century BC.*

Why is CERN called CERN?

Not long after the Second World War, scientists got together to rebuild research in Europe. They wanted to join their countries' resources to develop very expensive machines. They dreamed of a laboratory where scientists from all over Europe would study the infinitesimally small together. They thought it would be a way to consolidate peace. These scientists, from twelve countries, established a working group called the 'Conseil européen pour la recherche nucléaire', or the European Council for Nuclear Research. The acronym 'CERN' is derived from this name. At the time, the smallest known types of matter were the parts of atomic nuclei. The discipline was therefore called nuclear research, 'nuclear' being the adjective relating to the noun 'nucleus'. In 1954, this council established the European Organization for Nuclear Research, but the acronym CERN was kept. Since then, we've discovered even smaller parts of matter and a vast number of particles, and the discipline is now referred to as 'particle physics'.

> *One day, Oppenheimer told me of a problem that was very much on his mind... He believed that Europe's shaken nations did not have the resources to rebuild their basic physics infrastructure. He felt they would no longer be able to remain scientific leaders unless they pooled their money and talent.*

François de Rose, *on the birth of CERN, Nature, 2008*

Do researchers always use extraordinary machines in their experiments?

No, researchers don't always use extraordinary machines. They often use tools that already exist, such as pixels, like those in cameras. However, to discover new phenomena, you need to come up with experiments that have never been performed before and develop new experimental equipment, such as detectors. Researchers sometimes invent new technologies to do this. The technologies developed for experiments can have other immediate uses, and innovation in other fields also contributes to science. So, there's a constant back-and-forth between science and innovation, and therefore between science and society.

> About Anton Leeuwenhoek,
> the inventor of the microscope:
> Impossible! Most Dutchmen said.
> This Anton's crazy in the head!
> We ought to ship him off to Spain!
> He says he's seen a housefly's brain!
> He says the water that we drink
> Is full of bugs! He's mad, we think!
> They called him dumkopf, which means dope.
> That's how we got the microscope.

Maxim Kumin, *The Microscope*, 1984

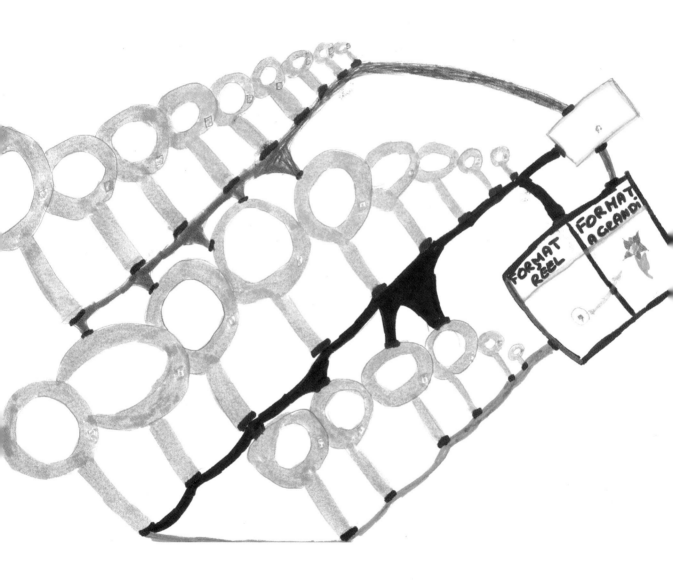

Why do we need a large machine to look at something very small?

The bigger the machine, the easier it is to see small things. With CERN's LHC machine, which measures 27 km in circumference, and its detectors, we can see what's inside matter with a precision of a billionth of a billionth of a metre. It's the best microscope in the world! For the time being, quarks and electrons are the smallest known components of the matter that surrounds us. Only with a very large machine can we see them and find out what's inside them!

> *Vidocq, for example, was a good guesser, and a persevering man. But, without educated thought, he erred continually by the very intensity of his investigations. He impaired his vision by holding the object too close.*

Edgar Allan Poe,
The Murders in the Rue Morgue, 1841

What will physicists do when they've discovered what's inside particles?

The smallest types of matter that we've discovered so far are quarks and electrons. Are these elementary particles, or are they composed of even smaller particles? Physicists are pondering this question and trying to observe them even more closely to see whether they're made up of even smaller parts. To do this, they need to build increasingly powerful machines that can help search for smaller and smaller things.

"*The world is clear water in a china bowl. You may clutch the bowl in your hands, but you will never seize the clear water.*"
"*I can dip my fingers in, or drink it,*" *replied Reb Seidel.*
"*What for?,*" *said Reb Noual then.* "*Your fingers would dry immediately, and your thirst be quenched but for a moment.*"
And he concluded:
Thirst is our lot.

Edmond Jabès, *The Book of Questions*, 1973

● Photon

● Gluon

• Gluon

● Positron

Why is it useful to see very small things?

Electrons were discovered at the end of the nineteenth century. Atoms were discovered at the beginning of the twentieth century. At the time, these were the smallest known things in the universe. Researchers learned to understand how they worked, but we didn't think we'd be able to use them for anything. However, electrons are the basis for electricity, and the mechanics of atoms allow us to make radios, mobile phones, and medicines. We don't yet know what we might be able to do with quarks, but perhaps we'll find a use for them in the future.

"

Knowing the force and action of fire, water, air, the stars, the heavens, and all the other bodies that surround us, as distinctly as we know the various crafts of our artisans, we might also apply them in the same way to all the uses to which they are adapted, and thus render ourselves the lords and possessors of nature.

"

René Descartes, *Discourse on the Method, 1637*

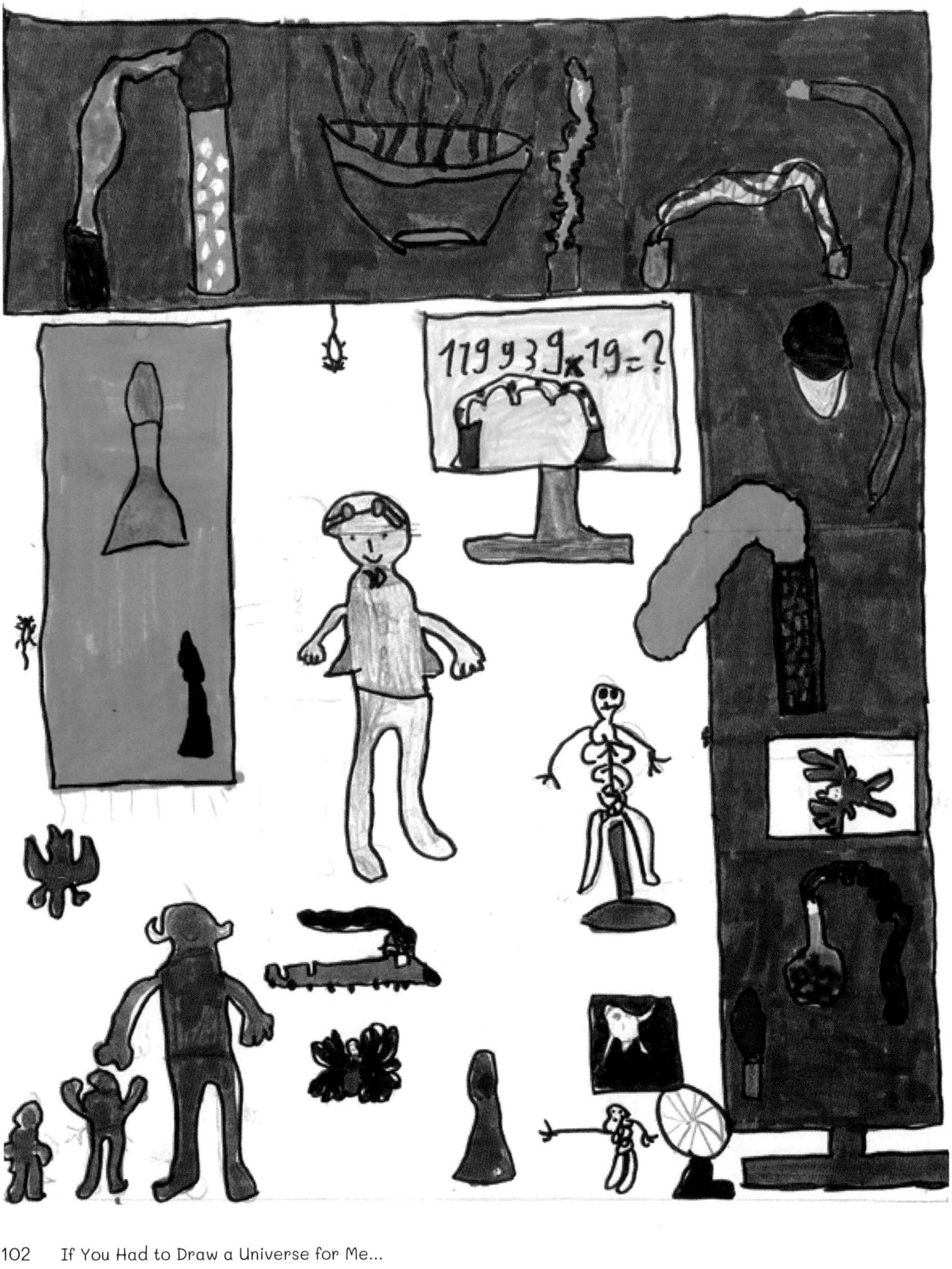
119939x19=?

Has CERN been able to answer the question of where mankind came from?

CERN, with its 10,000 researchers from all over the world, is trying to understand what matter is made of and how it formed 13.8 billion years ago, just after the Big Bang. But CERN isn't trying to answer the question of how humans appeared on Earth several million years ago. That is a question for archaeologists, palaeontologists, and biologists.

> When, while the Earth was opening her petals,
> The first man uttered the first word, that word,
> Born from his lips, and heard by everything,
> Met Light in heaven, and said to her:
> "Fly off,
> Sister! illumine stars, soar, be eternal,
> And fill all eyes forever! Warm the skies,
> The spheres and blazing globes,
> And light the outside, as I light the inside."

Victor Hugo, *Contemplations*, 1856

Is science dangerous for humans?

Scientific research brings us new knowledge about the world around us. But does this new knowledge bring only benefits? This is still a subject of much debate. On the one hand, advances in knowledge have allowed us to raise our standard of living, improve our comfort, fight many diseases and increase lifespan. On the other hand, they haven't helped us to reduce inequality or conflict. The development of new technologies, made possible by knowledge, brings with it not only benefits but also risks for humanity, such as new weapons and pollution.

Scientists aren't the only ones responsible for how we use new knowledge. The human race and its communities share this responsibility.

> *Learn from me, if not by my precepts, at least by my example, how dangerous is the acquirement of knowledge, and how much happier that man is who believes his native town to be his world, than he who aspires to become greater than his nature will allow.*

Mary Shelley, *Frankenstein, 1818*

Has anyone ever been teleported?

Teleportation is the instant transportation of an object from one place to another. So far, the only thing we've been able to teleport is the disembodied state — in other words, the characteristics — of a particle, or even of an atom, which is a small group of particles. For example, we've managed to teleport, and thus instantly transfer, the characteristics of one gold atom onto another gold atom a metre away. For now, teleporting particles, complex objects, and above all human beings seems beyond our reach. It's not impossible, however — for particles, at least.

> *Genie, said Aladdin, I call thee, to command thee, on the part of thy mistress, this lamp here, to transport this palace presently into China, to the same place from whence it was brought hither...*
>
> *Immediately the palace was transported into China; which was only to be felt by two little shocks, the one when it was lifted up, the other when set down, and both in a short interval of time.*

Aladdin; or, The Wonderful Lamp

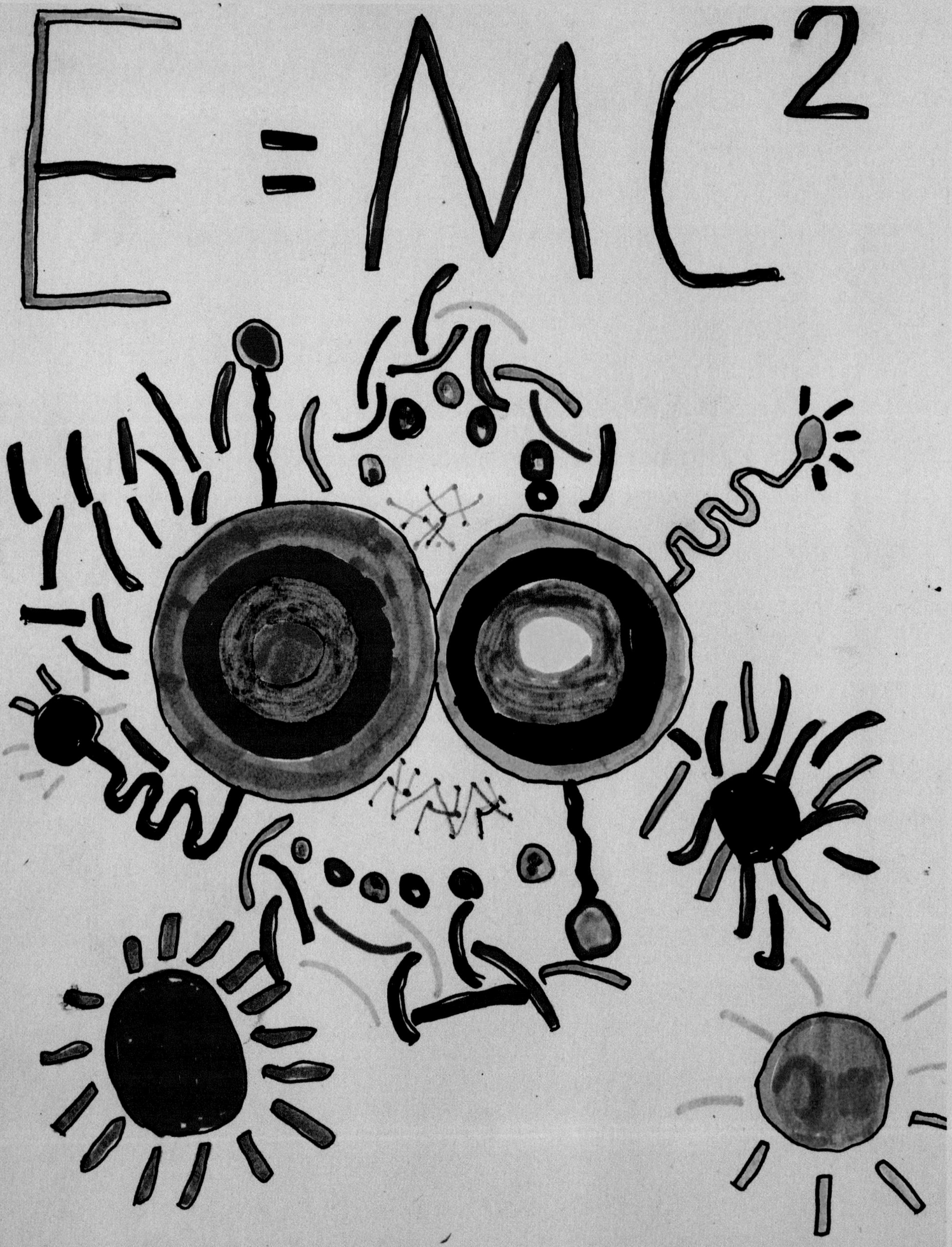
E = MC²

Why don't the laws of physics change?

Everything in the universe changes and evolves. Matter evolved out of a primordial soup of particles to become more complex. The stars evolved. Life appeared and evolved. But everything obeys the laws of physics, which seem to have been the same forever, throughout the universe! What are they made of? Could they change one day? Are they part of the world? Are they a separate world, or were they created by humans to help them understand the world? These questions have haunted scientists and philosophers for a long time.

> *Philosophy is written in this grand book, the universe, which stands continually open to our gaze. But the book cannot be understood unless one first learns to comprehend the language and read the characters in which it is written. It is written in the language of mathematics, and its characters are triangles, circles, and other geometrical figures.*

Galileo, *The Assayer*, 1623

Our little contributors

Translated words in illustrations

p. 86	*classeurs*	folders
p. 88	*j'ai gagné*	I've won
	je suis le meilleur	I'm the best
	poubelle	bin
	grosse étincelle	big sparks
	plouf plaf	splish splash
p. 94	*auto-destruction*	self-destruct
p. 96	*format réel*	real size
	format agrandi	enlarged
p. 98	*ordinateur du CERN*	CERN computer
	azote liquide	liquid nitrogen
	au CERN je CERN le problème	at CERN I disCERN the problem
	fiole	flask
p. 104	*huile*	oil
	butane	butane
	alcool	alcohol
	azote	nitrogen
	gants	gloves

Published by

WS Education, an imprint of

World Scientific Publishing Co. Pte. Ltd.

5 Toh Tuck Link, Singapore 596224

USA office: 27 Warren Street, Suite 401-402, Hackensack, NJ 07601

UK office: 57 Shelton Street, Covent Garden, London WC2H 9HE

Names: Goldberg, Marc (Physicist), author.
Title: If you had to draw a universe for me ... / Marc Goldberg (CERN, Switzerland) [and
Other titles: Si tu devais me dessiner l'univers. English
Description: New Jersey : World Scientific, 2018. | Audience: Age 7–12. |
    Originally published in French: Si tu devais me dessiner l'univers : 50 questions sur l'u
    la matière, les chercheurs pour le primaire (Paris : Editions le Pommier, 2015).
Identifiers: LCCN 2018040045 | ISBN 9789813277212 (pbk.)
Subjects: LCSH: Astronomy--Juvenile literature | Outer space--Juvenile literature. |
    Cosmology--Juvenile literature. | Children's questions and answers.
Classification: LCC QB46 .S525413 2018 | DDC 520--dc23
LC record available at https://lccn.loc.gov/2018040045

British Library Cataloguing-in-Publication Data
A catalogue record for this book is available from the British Library.

For any available supplementary material, please visit
https://www.worldscientific.com/worldscibooks/10.1142/11182#t=suppl

Editor: Daniele Lee
Designer: Jimmy Low

Printed in Singapore

3 8001 00138 5446